TURNING WITHIN

Thomas Johnson-Medland

TURNING WITHIN

*An Introductory
Manual of Meditation
for Christians in the World*

by
Thomas Johnson-Medland,
(Deacon Athanasios)

PRAXIS INSTITUTE PRESS

Praxis Institute Press
5, Devon Place, Totnes TQ9 5AE
Devon, England.

Copyright Thomas Johnson-Medland and Praxis Research Institute Inc. No work may reproduce more than 10% of this book in any form without permission from the publisher but permission is granted for inclusions of up to 10% of the text if credited to Praxis.

First impression 1998

British Library Cataloguing in Publication Data:
A catalogue record for this book is available from the British Library.
Medland, Thomas.
Turning Within.

ISBN 1-872292-21-6

Printed in England by Booksprint

Acknowledgements:

For Glinda, my beloved wife; Zoe, my angelic daughter (of blessed memory); and Zachary, my sweet son. You are my little Trinity, my community of love, my place of peace, my dwelling. Thank you - Thomas

We acknowledge our gratitude to those members of Praxis Research Institute, of the Tenth Man School in Texas, of the Community of Saint Antony and Saint Elias and to D.A.B. Lenney in the United Kingdom, for the help which over the years has made it possible for us to produce our publications and to keep them in front of the public on four continents.

"How can I explain who the One is who is joined to me and to whom I am joined, I who have become one? I am frightened. I am afraid that if I tell you, you will doubt and fall into blasphemy as a result of your ignorance. Nonetheless, having become one being, I and the One to whom I am joined, what name shall I give myself? The God who has two natures united in one person has made a double being of me. Having made me double, He therefore has given me two names. Behold the difference! By nature I am a man; by grace I am God."
(Saint Symeon the New Theologian.)

PUBLISHER'S PREFACE

"Behold, I stand at the door, and knock: if any man hear my voice, and open the door, I will come in to him, and will sup with him, and he with me." (Revelations 3:20.)

In this book you will not meet the voice of dogma or intellectual theology, yet here, in these few pages, some of us will find a familiar voice, as well as some of the most simple yet most penetrating advice on what is sometimes called 'interior prayer' ever given first in the English language. For those who can hear, it is a book that knocks on the door of the heart.

In the world of the Orthodox, religious experience still sometimes transcends life, penetrating beyond the boundary of death in ways that awaken faith and feed the flame of hope. In this way, prayer penetrates into the individual, awakening the same faith and feeding the same hope until some joyous fusion awakens in the prepared soul the voice of that Spirit of God once known to the early fathers who shaped that Eastern church.

Thomas Johnson-Medland is an American. He is also a deacon of the Orthodox church; a husband and father of a child, whose work is to care for the dying in a New Jersey hospice. In his life, service and prayer have met in a splendid fusion that he will not wish me to speak of. As publisher,

I have sought to overrule his wish on this one point, because I must. I must do so if I can simply because it will reveal the combined power of these two so innocent factors, and this will make visible the value of giving more time given to the awakening of true spirituality in a world which in general gives little time to spirit. Here, indeed, we might say that time has been sacrificed to the service of God, in prayer and charity, and in living the gospel inwardly as well as outwardly.

When I first received this manuscript I was delighted to see it. When my parish priest, Father Benedict Ramsden, saw the manuscript, it obviously struck him in the same way, so that he and his community of St.Anthony and St.Elias have played an important role in encouraging us to take the opportunity to put this remarkable work into print.

Now, reading it a number of times, I have found that it - and its author - have become familiar friends, as well as harbingers of that invisible presence known in some parts of the East as 'the Friend.' But this is not all. Small though the book is, it goes deep, and as it plunges into the depths of spirit it touches on many of the most important questions of interior prayer and explains with simple and warm clarity practical aspects of prayer that have in many places been forgotten for five hundred years.

Robin Amis

INTRODUCTION

I am not able or worthy to be a teacher in our faith. For I am a sinner. I hurt people and I am hurt by them. I tell lies and I spread rumours. I think thoughts that I should not think, and do things I should not do. I do not fast properly and I do not pray as often as I should. Often, I tear people down, rather than build them up. I do not come to the Holy Mysteries when I should, and I profane God by continuing to be a sinner even after coming to their awesome power. I am a sinner.

But l have found a great joy in this rotting flesh. I have found a place in the heart that radiates sheer ecstasy and bliss. I want to tell you about this. For, in this person, who all day walks around devising one more way to make himself better and higher than others - one more way to get what he wants - there lives the very God of all, the pre-existing One, the One from all ages to all ages: the great I AM. The Ultimate Reality exists in this sinner.

I have been graced with the opportunity to meet Him in the stillness of my heart. I do not know why I have been able other than that I have looked for him there for many years. It certainly is not because I am a worthy vessel. Perhaps I am just persistent It is as if my self-effort has met His grace, and the fruit of this union is Paradise within.

I have noticed that our Orthodox Faith has become a place of anger and hostility. It is subtly woven into this tapestry of beauty, but do not miss its presence. When we attend the Liturgy, or workshops, or conferences, the theme tends to always get around to, *what we are doing right and all the other churches and faiths are doing wrong, and how we are better than all the rest - especially the catholics and protestants.* This is not really an issue for the one who sits in the presence of Jesus within.

This is not of major concern to Him who has become welded to the Divine. The one who is being divinized does not see the world with such fear, but he sees the ultimate triumph of unity within Him Who is the All in All. What becomes most central in the life of one who is in their heart and is in the heart of Jesus, is how to be more in the heart, and more, and more - how to remain always in the presence of Jesus.

To arrive at such a feeling of freedom and release is of course a process. It is a process of the Holy Spirit acting within the believer. It is a process that will go on by itself with only one form of food or input required of the believer. The believer must seek to become more and more aware of the actual Presence of the Divine One within. The believer must - as St. Seraphim said - *"Acquire the Holy Spirit"*. That is, unpack the reality of the fact that God dwells within us.

The Philokalia is filled with images of this process, so we are not set adrift without any help. We must, with Diadokos of Photiki, clean off the dirt from the image planted within us. We must remove ignorance from the mind (the *nous*, or 'eye' eye'eye of the soul') that we may see the heart - the place where Jesus lives. But, even though we have the guide-ropes of the Masters, there are very few living Masters who are practising this opening of the mind. In this journey, as with all journeys, we must begin with prayer. We must pray for the Holy Spirit to raise up men and women who are Masters of the Heart. We must pray for leaders who will show us salvation. We must pray for those who would come to bring a healing balm to us and teach us how to become by grace what Jesus is by nature… somehow one with all that is.

Perhaps, as we turn ourselves to absorbing more of God, the Church itself will return in glory to the beauty of its true nature as the very vessel and tabernacle of the One who is beyond all reason, beyond all prejudice, beyond all theology itself. Then the Church will become the bearer of God: Theotokos.

This is the life of the one who wishes to follow Jesus. We must become more and more like the Virgin. We must ponder what this means; to be a House of the Divine. We are a Palace of the Master. We are a Heavenly Tabernacle. We are a Womb for Jesus.

Meditation is sitting, turning the attention within and looking for God in us. It is discerning who we really are. It is becoming conscious of reality. It is melting away the illusions of ignorance and finding that we are what we have been all along. It is no new thing for us Orthodox, but it is something lost to us Orthodox, especially in the West. We have turned ourselves away from it for so many years. The migration to America seems to have disturbed many things for our Church. We spend more time in jurisdictional battles and doctrinal debate than is healthy for a person, or for a Church. We look all bent and lopsided. We have lost our hearts.

It is time for us to reclaim our dignity as offspring of God. We must lay down all the hoopla and fingerpointing of the outer journey. In peace, let us pick up the tools of the Master and turn within. There we will do the work that really matters. There we will chip away traps of the mind and its friend the ego, and there we will discover the heart and open the eye of the soul. For the Heart is the hub. The Heart is the centre. The Heart is the Garden of Paradise. Let us go there and wander. In our wandering we will discover the opening of the eye of the soul, and we shall be made whole.

1. SIT

The greatest challenge to the inner journey is taking the first step. This journey, as all others, can begin only when we set out. Every day we must make time to go within. Every day we must struggle to look for Jesus in our heart.

At first, the way in which we do this turning within must be familiar and pleasant to us. If it is not, we will not wish to pursuit it. If it is not, we will not return to this practice with any regularity.

Find a quiet space in the home or around the house. Perhaps even a chapel, if there is one close at hand. It must be a place where you can get away from noise and people. Noise and people are very valuable for our lives, but without removing yourself from them in order to meditate, you will not become whole enough to live amid them in health. We must find our centre if we are to live in Jesus, for our centre is Jesus.

As humans, the majority of our physical life is based on a rhythmic repetition. We eat - several times each day, we breath several times each minute, we sleep, we empty ourselves of food and drink, we move, we work, etc. This routine seems to be part of what it means to be manifest in the physical world. This being the case, it makes sense that we must pass through the gate of rhythm if we are to enter Paradise. We must practice our meditation with regularity.

It is very easy to make the transition into a practice of meditation and then allow it to be the only form of piety we pursuit. This is not balanced, and it must be avoided. Therefore, when you sit for meditation, cross yourself, pray to our Lord and to His Mother, offer psalms, offer intercessions, petitions, to give thanks, and then enter into the process of meditation. This will keep you strong in the faith and keep you from marching down some zealous path of vainglory. Spirituality is not an easy path. It is a hard path. Meditation is no exception. We cannot find the King of All without a long hard journey. And, once we have found Him, we will not gain entrance to His Palace without offering him a gift - the gift of our self effort.

Things you may want to have in this quiet place are:

an icon of Jesus, the Trinity, or the Theotokos
a prayer book
a candle
a bible or Psalter
a prayer rope
a chair or cushion on the floor
incense
a tape player and relaxation music

When you come to this place, be sure you have eaten a light snack or meal, had a drink, used the facilities, unplugged the phone and taken care of any immediate business. Sit in your quiet place, make the sign of the cross, ask for a good beginning, and then make your attempt. At this time you should offer up whatever manner of prayers you are used to offering. When these are finished, you are ready to begin you meditation.

All of these things may seem silly to you. At the outset the rhythm is essential. Perhaps after ten years of practice you may go to a bus station and meditate while sitting in a line, but this is not how you should begin. After ten years of practice, you will easily be able to go to the sacred place within yourself, but at the beginning you must define the inner sacred space by having an outward sacred space. The path of growth is always inwards. It is always from the concrete to the intangible, from the iconic to the invisible. The movement in to the heart begins out here in the body.

Be firm with yourself for the first few years. Make sure you practice as many days as possible, and always get away into a sacred space, alone. Without this labour, you will not harvest the bounty when the crops have reached maturity,

Some of the Fathers recommend sitting on a chair, some cross legged, some sitting on your heels, and still others standing. I believe standing to meditate is for the adept and should not be your first choice. Sitting in a chair is by far the most moderate position, and this should be the starting place for everyone. It will keep you from becoming too zealous to look like someone who meditates and then burning out from expending all that energy trying to appear to be something you are not.

Later you can advance to sitting on the floor in a cross legged position, or on your heels. The goal should be to find a way that does not cause too much discomfort. We will be trying to steady and still the mind. The body will not let this happen if it feels too much discomfort. It will scream, "My legs are sore. I'm tired, let us sit down...."

Moderation will be right both for the body and the mind. This is as it should be.

You should be aware of the posture with which you hold yourself for prayer. Whenever you sit, pay attention to how you sit,. What does your physical posture tell you about your mental posture? If you slouch, or lean, or do not pay attention to how you are carrying, holding, or posturing yourself, what does this say about your spiritual development? First, hold the body in a good way. Then, you may move on to the mind. And only then may you move from the mind into the heart.

So, sit up. Straighten your spine. Lengthen your neck. Gently place your hands on your lap. Close your eyes. Repeat the Jesus Prayer and imagine yourself relaxing into your own sitting posture. *"Lord Jesus Christ, Son of God, have mercy on me a sinner (or Jesus have mercy)."*

QUOTES:

(On sitting on ones heels, coiled up, with one's chest on one's knees).

"Not only will man gather himself externally, conforming to an interior movement which he seeks for his spirit, but in giving such a posture to his body, he will send toward the interior of the heart the power of the spirit which flows out to the exterior ..... the spirit comes back on itself, its movement is circular, which is its proper activity."

- *Saint Gregory Palamas*

"Sit with the body straight and the shoulders at ease. Be like a violin string tuned to the right note, without too much tension too much slackness."

Saint Theophan the Recluse

2. FOCUS THE MIND, FOCUS THE HEART

It is true, beyond a shadow of a doubt, the mind is both the best of friends and the worst of enemies. And, because it is the mind which surrounds the heart, protecting it and hiding it at the same time, we must become familiar with the mind before we can enter into the heart. The mind is a great and awesome mirror, able to reflect all things.

Many people do not realise the role and function of the mind. Because of this, they are never at peace with the mind, and are unable to work with their mind so as to enter into the heart. When the mind encases the heart and keeps it safe from attack, it also keeps its contents hidden from us. Most things function in this type of dichotomy. It is the balance of things that makes our Orthodox Faith so strong.

Just as we are on a great quest and journey to find God, we are also on a quest to open our heart and reveal its contents. The mind contains thoughts and impressions from the material world. The heart contains feelings and intuitions which come from a non-material foundation.

God has used the mind to conceal Himself. God hides behind the mind. God is hiding behind our mind because we have chosen to raise it up in order to obtain the fruit of the Tree of the Knowledge of Good and Evil. God hides behind our mind because He wants us to search for Him as the Lover seeks the Beloved

The mind is where most of us have chosen to dwell. The mind is the organ of the human personality we most readily identify ourselves with. We believe we are what we think and perceive. We make decisions based on all of the external data we can gather. This is not the fullest potential we people can attain to. We live in the head, which is where we think the mind dwells.

Although the head is the seat of the mind, the mind is not limited to this place alone. The mind runs throughout all of the body. This is because of its intimate connection with the senses.

We can move into the heart. We can identify ourselves with the organ that feels and intuits. This is a movement in people who have made a 'drop' into the heart, that is, people who operate more readily from their heart than from their mind. These people are much more relaxed and make us feel very welcome. We feel welcome with them because they have not only integrated into their minds all the information they have been able to gather from their senses - but they have been able to add to it the feelings and impressions that bubble up from within them. They are fuller people, and much more aware.

Further in than either the mind or the heart is the eye of the soul. It is our very identity in God.

It is where there is no other reality than I AM. It is very common for all of us to enter into the eye of the soul for small portions of time. Very few people finally come to live in this place within themselves. All of them are considered saints. And yet, all of us are called to go to this place and so to have our hearts and minds fully transformed, or fully integrated.

Watchfulness is what the saints call the kind of attention it takes to keep our awareness in the eye of the soul all of the time. When we are this watchful, then we shall dwell in paradise continually. Until then, we shall only gather glimpses.

If we are attentive to it, the movement of life is always calling us further into ourselves. God has clothed our nakedness with our mind, and has Himself hidden Himself behind this clothing. This hiding is because of our desire to be self-conscious - wanting to be independent and living in the ego - and it is because of God's desire to draw and lure us back to Himself, both at once. God calls us back into our own centre, into our own heart. This is where we will meet Him - in the heart. And, even further in, we shall enter into the eye of the soul and become one with His Energies.

The eye of the soul is God's dwelling. It is the organ of our own Divine identity. It looks both inwardly and outwardly. When we have reached it and become one with it (or opened it), then we have begun the work of salvation and divinization.

This is the great portent of the images of the treasure hidden within a field, the pearl of great price, the finding of the widow's coin and the Tree of Life in the centre of Paradise. When we seek to find God with all of our being, it is in the cave of the heart that we find Him. God dwells within us. God dwells in our hearts. Because of this assumption, spirituality asserts that the spiritual journey is to become that which we already are. To become by Grace (by the discovery of God within us) what Christ is by Nature (God in Flesh).

When we remove all ignorance and wrong thinking and realise the truth that God is already there - but that it is we who must uncover this glory - then we can recognise the true beauty, joy and bliss of the spiritual path of theosis. It is a continual meeting of God in us. It is God revealing God to Himself. We are the joy of the realisation and the revelation of the Divine. We are the ground upon which God reveals Himself.

But it is the mind that has free will. The mind can either reflect the glory of the heart outward through the senses onto all that is, or, reflect the passion of the senses inward onto the heart. It can let God leak out to divinize all He touches, or it can let the lesser rays of light - the passions - trickle into the core of our existence and taint and darken the image within. We identify our lives either with an inward pulling motion or an outward going motion. We collect from our senses in to our centre, or we allowing the heart to shape all our views of the world and thus sanctify our senses.

The mark of spiritual development is the continual circular motion of the life-energies - a pulling in of images so that they may be sanctified in the heart. Then they can be sent back out to the physical world around us - divinized. This can only happen when the eye of the soul is opened and our watchfulness and attention rests in it - whether continually, or only periodically.

The mind is the centre for collecting and interpreting all the data perceived by the senses. We see something happen; the eyes absorb the sight and send it to the mind. The mind catalogues it. We hear something happen; the ears absorb the sound and send it to the mind. The mind catalogues it. And so, little by little, the mind collects information about the external world and stores it away, learning to make assumptions about how the world functions based on its interpretation of the steady stream of images that the senses feed it. The mind is a mirror reflecting all that the senses have gathered.

But, there is another side to the mind. The mind also reflects God. God dwells in the heart, and the mind is able to also reflect what it gathers from the heart. If the mind is focused, so that it is stilled and quieted and turned within, it can reflect the glory of its identity in God. The mind is capable of reflecting God's compassion and so teaching the hands and feet to pick up bread for the poor and carry it to them. The heart can reflect the joy of God and teach the hands to clap and the feet to dance when someone is born. The mind is capable of reflecting the Divine uncreated Light within us and so bringing Light to a darkened world.

We are capable of reflecting or imaging in either direction. We can reflect - on the mind - the images we see, hear, taste, touch, and smell all around us, or we can reflect - also on the mind - the image of the Divine One within. This is where we see the imagery of the creation versus the Creator that we find in Saint Paul and the Fathers of the Church. The Creator is at our core.

If we allow the Creator in the heart to be reflected onto the mind and then trickle out to all our senses, so shaping the way we touch, taste, smell, see, and hear, then we allow God to become manifest in the world. On the other hand, if we allow the mind only to reflect the data of the world around it, we build layer upon layer of sensory illusion that collects around the heart and so makes it a 'heart of stone' - trapping the Divine within it.

All of the things we store in the mind - everything about how the world is, everything recorded by the senses - all of these things will reappear when we begin to meditate.

And all these images that we collect around the heart will eventually have to be burned away when we wish to approach the heart by stilling the mind.

If you have tried to sit for meditation, you will already be familiar with the way the mind operates. You will have heard it say: 'What should I do? Am I sitting right? Why did they say that to me? Did I put all the dishes away? Are they really going to do what they said they would? Should I have fed the cat earlier? I remember the colour of that flower; it was a deep orange with yellow streaks. The dog was really acting strangely this morning; perhaps he is ill. I know the weather report called for sun, but I think it is going to rain.' There is a good chance we will have to rifle through millions of sensory images before the mind can begin to settle and become still.

This is the unfocused mind. It is scattered, and there is no order to the images that arise, no control over the images that arise. It moves from one thing to the next. It may take many years of sitting with your eyes closed, and repeating the Jesus Prayer, before these millions of images cease to arise. What is the rush? Remember, at the centre of it all is God. Thank Him for this. And sit.

The mind will find all manner of external imagery to focus on. First, perhaps, there will be an immense list of questions it asks. Each question will be attached to a collection of picture images, which will systematically present themselves inside you and offer feelings of contentment or distress to you. You may be content to watch the images, or distressed at not being able to suppress them.

This is usual. The mind is restless. It has stored many reflections of the world of the senses: many images of the external field. But the mind alone cannot enable us to find a way to live. The mind has no way of sorting out all the data it perceives ... except on the basis of the data it has already perceived. It does not know its own purpose. Only the Divine One, located in the heart, can reveal the purpose of all that the mind perceives. The mind has no centre of its own. The heart is the centre.

Watching all of these things, however, will help you to realise that you have a mind. You live in your mind most of the time. Your mind is full. Yet your mind is not the source of life ... there must be more. This quest for more is sometimes called turning within, or turning to God. It is the only action we can commit that will bring us to grace. This is our sole self-effort: to turn ourselves toward God.

So, we sit. By sitting, we turn ourselves toward God. We discover our mind and its limitations, and so we say there must be more. We turn ourselves more toward God. We discover the heart.

Some people allow their minds to be the centre. They make decisions based on the limited scope of what their own mind has catalogued from the perceptions of their senses. This is limited knowledge. This limited knowledge is valuable for keeping us alive as beasts, but it does not enable us to move on, to reach our divine status. However, this is how most people live their lives: centred on their mind.

People will call up information the mind has stored, allow the mind to sort through it, interpret it, and then make decisions based on it. The mind is capable of doing this, but this is not the Source of Life and does not always reflect the Source of Life. In other words, some people live just from collecting information and then acting. They do not question how they are able to do this. They do not question where the mind gets its ability to do this. They do not ask who is it who is interpreting all this mind-stuff.

On and on the mind goes, racing. It makes connections here and there with the small bits of facts that have been fed to it by the senses. This aspect of the mind goes out of the body through the senses and so it perceives the world around it. It is not still, and it cannot be still. This function of the mind is to help the body survive and to keep it from harm. This is why we do everything we do. Ultimately, we use the mind in its outward flowing activity to keep us alive. It helps us learn and make a living. It helps us shop and cook our food. It helps us drive the car and arrive at our destinations. This outward flowing activity of the mind is geared toward DOING, and DOING is for surviving. The outward flow of the mind is very much for the body and its life.

But there is also a forgotten task of the mind. This forgotten task is the inward flowing activity of the mind. The mind can reflect what is already inside it. The mind can reflect our BEING. And, when it reflects our BEING, it is reflecting the presence of God in the heart - the NOUS. The inward flow of the mind is very much for the whole life of an individual, for it is this which us able to integrate the needs of our body, as well as able to accommodate our whole to divinization.

The mind must be active to reflect what is going on in the world of DOING. But the mind must be stilled to reflect the world of BEING. It is in the BEING of the heart that the doing of the mind through the body is made holy and kept in line with TRUTH.

Only if we still the mind can we look at the heart and begin to reflect the presence of God onto the world . For this stilling of the mind, we must have a technique.

There are many techniques used to still the mind, but all of them revolve around the notion of harnessing the mind by focusing it. We focus the mind by the use of repetition. For some, it may be repetition of a sound, while for others it may be the repetition of a thought, a sight, a smell or a feeling. Repetition enables the mind to grab hold of one thing and then focus itself to stillness.

Repetition for the eyes would be to gaze on an icon or a candle. Repetition for the ears would be to hear a melody over and over again. Repetition for the mouth would be to recite the Jesus Prayer without end. Repetition for the mind itself would be the repetition within of an idea or a story. Whatever the technique, it should be begun outside, in the body, and then moved inside, into the mind. This means staring at an icon and then closing the eyes and seeing it within. This means repeating the name of Jesus vocally, and then silently closing the mouth and repeating it within. Move the repetitious activity from outside to inside. Repeat it inside, and this will help the mind become still.

This process will not happen overnight. You cannot begin today and expect that by tomorrow the mind will make the transition from outward repetition of the name of Jesus to the interior repetition, and then become completely still. This will take years. But this is where the practice must begin. As you practice it, you will begin to understand the mind, and then you will become able to work with it.

Once this happens, as the mind becomes still through constant practice, you will then be able to see the heart; the mind will then reflect the contents of the heart. At first the mind will reflect darkness, and then the mind will reflect light. Both light and darkness are the reflection of the presence of the Divine One; the reflection of Jesus in the heart. Light or darkness, it does not matter, the shift in awareness or perception from the mind (generally identified by its location in the head), to the heart (as the centre of the chest cavity) is the mark that we have moved into the heart. This movement will be accompanied first by darkness, then by the reflection of the heart on the mind. After this is watched for a time, the lights will disappear and darkness will again reappear. The shift to the heart should be felt soon after this.

This movement from many images to stillness and then to darkness, to light, and then again to darkness, is the movement of life. Life pulsates, it is not static. The fathers call us to move from seeing lights to not seeing them because the ultimate place where we will end up is in a place that has no images. This place is pure being, pure heaven. This place will be the eye of the soul. The eventual goal will be to hold our awareness of our BEING, to hold our awareness of this place in ourselves: to always remember God: mneme Theou.

Let me say it again. Whether you see lights or darkness it does not matter. There is light and darkness in the mind, there is light and darkness in the heart. God is in both. It is the shift of awareness that marks the movement into the heart.

When you feel your sense of centre or identity go from the head to the heart, then you are in the heart. Ultimately the feeling of a pinpoint awareness in the centre of the heart is the movement from the heart to the eye of the soul.

Any movement within, will happen briefly at first and then become more consistent and eventually constant. That is, for several minutes you will feel your awareness in the heart, and then it will go back into the head again. Then, after six months it will last longer. One day the awareness may just take up permanent residence in the heart and radiate out from there. Then you will begin to experience a deeper awareness in the eye of the soul, and so on.

There is no way to weld these concepts to your being without sitting and practising meditation. Without trial and error; and the concerted effort of a disciplined silent life, you will never know how the mind and the heart operate, how they are different organs and yet the same. Without the experience of turning within, you will not be able to identify the presence of the Kingdom within. There is no learning of the details here. Here there is only practice.

QUOTES

"When the mind is simple, or rather devoid of all concepts and completely clothed in the simple light of God, and hidden within it, the mind can find no other object to which it can direct the movement of its thought except the One in which it is anchored. It therefore remains in the abyss of the divine light which does not allow it to see anything outside of it." - Saint Symeon the New Theologian

"The mind which is always in motion becomes motionless and entirely empty of thought when it is covered completely by the divine darkness and the light. It lives a life beyond life, being a light within a light, but not a light to itself, for it is not itself whom it sees, but Him who is above it, and the glory coming from Him makes the mind a stranger to its own thought, so it no longer knows itself as a thinking mind." - Saint Symeon the New Theologian

3. GO WITHIN

The path of the interior life is fraught with many obstacles, challenges, and hurdles. Most difficult of all is the actual practice of meditation itself: Sitting down to turn within on a regular basis.

If you will sit every day - or every other - and be attentive to what is going on inside you, you will find the path. For attentiveness is the path. The inner spiritual life is not in what you see in meditation, so much as it is in the fact that you are watching, and sitting in the Presence of the Divine One. The aim of our sitting and of our focusing the mind is to become still and attentive. The aim of our sitting is Being. And in our Being, we will Become.

When we have attained a measure of stillness and attentiveness, then we will have shifted our perception from our earthly idea of self and mind and heart into the heavenly idea of the same, In the heavenly, or interior way of understanding these things, God permeates all things. He is not separated from things. Although His nature is distinct, He is within all life'. When we have a universal vision of the presence of God - that is, when we see God as being in all places and in all things - then we will have attained a good thing. This is a pearl of great price.

So to attain spiritual stillness, we must sit. We must focus the mind using a device: the Jesus Prayer, an Icon, a sound, chant, a candle, etc. And we must watch. We must still the mind by constant repetition. Repetition of the practice of sitting. Repetition of the name of Jesus. Repetition of watching the mind. Repetition of moving into the heart. Walk down the path each day and you will move further and further along it, move further and further toward its end.

It helps to see yourself as the one who views all that occurs, instead of as the one doing all the things you imagine. That is, when you are meditating and the idea comes to "let the dog out", think of it differently, as, "my mind wants me to let the dog out." When the thought arises "it is time to eat breakfast", the attentive one sees it as, "a thought has arisen to eat breakfast." In watching the thoughts that arise in the mind, you will be helping rid the mind of its chaotic activity, and this helps the mind become still. The mind must learn that it is just one organ of our Identity, it is not our Identity. When the mind is still, our awareness settles into the heart. This is where the great light of God resides. Here, in the heart, we will be closer to our real Identity

Then this notion of "I" will become central to your inner growth. At first, like everyone, you will see yourself as body or as mind. In truth, the I is influenced by these things, but it is the ruler of them. Ultimately, we are seeking to transform the mind and the body. For this we need the Divine Light of the heart - which is hidden in the depths of the Nous. This can only transform us if we see ourselves as the observer of the mind, the body, and the heart.

To see this is attentiveness. This is what it means to be attentive. It is to see yourself as distinct from the body, the mind, and the heart, and yet intimately a part of them. To see this is to have the eye of the soul opened. This is the basis of Trinitarian theology.

Everything that emerges, everything that arises, will be reflected on the mirror of the mind. The mind mirrors its contents. So images that arise, whether verbal, mental, visual, audible, or tactile, will be arising out of the mind and projected onto the mind. These images will continue to come until the collection of images with which the mind has surrounded the heart have worn themselves down and there are no more things that block the heart so that it is not directly projected onto the mind. When this is so, you will see light.

Once the light has been seen and the awareness drops into the heart, then the process begins again. The images of the heart arise. They will project themselves on the heart until all of the images have been cut through, so that the eye of the soul can be seen. There will be light, and then darkness. The shift of awareness will go inward at this point. Before this shift occurs, you will feel pain in the heart region. Then there will be the feeling of the heart collapsing into itself in an eternal fall of grace.

Remember, we are always cautioned away from the light, because it is easy to think this beautiful place is the end. This is not the end. The Fathers pushed us away from here because they did not want us to get stuck here. It is dangerous to think the light is all there is. It is the same as in the theology of the Icon and of the Image, where the goal is to move from the image to the imageless, the tangible to the intangible. We use images and light in order to be able to grasp the true nature. That true nature is ungraspable, uncontainable. Light and image are here to carry us to a place where they themselves do not exist.

Then you will be in the eye of the soul. The feeling of bliss is here. The sense of BEING is here. This is the I AM. You will feel a sense of disorientation and complete rest.

Diadokos of Photiki called this process of shifting from head to heart to the eye of the soul "the removal of the dirt from the canvas painting of the Holy Spirit". It is the slow and steady process of revitalising the Image of God in us by removing false impressions and obstacles to that Image. The things that stand between us and our own heart, between us and God, may not be evil things in and of themselves, but in so much as we see them as objects that are separate from us and God, and do not see that they are permeated with us and God, then they are not participating in the Divinization of all creation. This process occurs when we visit the Image of God in us often enough to enable us to be transformed into His Likeness.

Technically, within the Orthodox Tradition, the thing that sees the images projected on the mind, (as well as those ruminated on and stored in the heart), is called the NOUS. This is the eye of the soul. In terms of the placement of this organ, it is within the mind, within the heart. It is the true Self. It has the potential to witness all that occurs. It may look outward through the heart, the mind, and the organs of the mind - the body and its senses being one of those organs; or it may look inward to the fullness of the Kingdom.

When it looks within, it feeds upon Itself and is full and content and needs no other thing. This is the enlightenment of the Fathers, and this is the return to Paradise. It is union with God.

I say, 'technically' because it takes many years for the student of meditation to be able to identify that there is a distinction between the mind, the heart and the eye of the soul. They really are all one organ, and they really are three separate organs, but this dichotomy is very difficult to place for the beginner. If this is too hard to understand, just place this information in the heart and allow it to grow there, then it may emerge for you during a period of understanding.

This is the mark of how an object, or person, or image is participating in our process of Theosis: If we see them as Divinized - a part of God - then we are connected to our heart in this matter. If we do not identify these things as a part of God, there is some measure of duality in our thinking toward the matter. I am not saying that all things are in the Essence of the Triune. I am saying all things are permeated with the Energies of the Thrice Holy. If we do not see this (visually or interiorly), then we are not quite on the mark in regard to that particular object/incident/creation.

The whole purpose of turning within is to focus the mind, to enter into the heart and open the eye of the soul, and, (for lack of words to describe this quest), to sit there in the Presence of the Ground of our Being - God. This is meditation. This is the inner spiritual path. This is the way of the heart.

If you are having problems focusing the mind and watching the images that emerge, perhaps you can take counsel from the Fathers of the Philokalia and imagine the mind draining - down from its seat in the head into the heart. Imagine it as a pouring of the contents of the mind into the chest. Doing this simple exercise will take you further into a stillness.

This practice may take years to perfect. It may not make sense for years, but practising it will help it become a reality.

A large danger on the spiritual path is the urge to rush grace. Our job is to make our self-effort daily We cannot demand results, stillness, or a feeling of inner connection to God. Grace comes from God. God will meet our self-effort with His grace. This is how we grow.

I would like to turn special and specific attention to the use of the Jesus Prayer - the Prayer of the Heart - at this time. The repetition of the sweetest name of Jesus (*"LORD Jesus, have mercy on me"* - or- "LORD Jesus Christ, Son of God, have mercy on me a sinner" - or - *"Jesus, have mercy"*) is the surest path into the heart. This is because Jesus is not only the path, but the very attainment and goal of the path. The whole spiritual life is permeated with Jesus, for He is the spiritual path itself. Life in God is about becoming - by Grace - what Jesus is by Nature, namely, God and Man. Jesus is All in All.

The prayer has come from centuries of practice and refinement along the spiritual journey.. The Fathers and Mothers of the Eastern Christian Tradition, have worked with contemplation, meditation, and this prayer, in great zeal. I do not wish to give a detailed history here of the rise of this prayer, for others have done this with greater accuracy than could I. My concern, here, is to establish the Jesus Prayer as the most mystic and invincible weapon of the Christian Meditator.

Sitting, armed with the Jesus Prayer, the believer who wishes to turn within and find mystic union with God has the most sacred ally and support. The key is to be consistent. Sit, pray the prayer, seeking all the while to turn within, and watch. For there is one deep inside you who is watching all this. This knower is your true Identity. This knower is the eye of God and the eye of the soul: the one place where both of these things come together.

It takes years of practice to make any advance. This is designed to keep the less serious from entering into the sacred realms. To go within and yet not be prepared to give up your very identity is a hazard. Countless tales of madness come out of the desert warning us to not take the inner journey lightly. Therefore, countless years of testing your intent are necessary. This is why we sit with daily regularity. We must show the heart that we want to see God, and that we are willing to be patient and earnest.

Prelest, or falling prey to illusions of greatness, is a great foe on the inner journey. While sitting and practicinq the prayer, and turning within, we will do countless hours of battle with this demon. The only thing that will keep us on the path and victorious over this demon is if we persevere; if we do not give up because we feel 'nothing is happening'. Everything we do when we turn toward Jesus and utter His name, becomes a piece of the great path that leads us home to our heart and to the presence of God. Do not listen to the whispers that tell us to give up. Persevere.

If our journey in is marked by a steady and growing feeling of unworthiness and repentance, then we shall be sure we are on the right path. I have fallen off the path by wishing to reveal these things to you in order to encourage you. I am unworthy to even speak about these things of which I know nothing.

Pray for a worthy teacher to come to you and guide you. But, remember, this will not come overnight. This will come in God's timing. All eternity exists for this process. Wait and be diligent.

QUOTES

"Since the Divine Nature is inaccessible, it is also inconceivable, and what is inconceivable is also inexpressible in every way. Among men and angels, who could have the power to explain the Invisible and Inconceivable? Absolutely no one, for that which Is not something cannot be imagined by human thought or signified by a word." - Saint Symeon the New Theologian

"The increase of our knowledge of God becomes the cause and the reason for our ignorance of all other beings, including God Himself. The Immensity of His Light leads to the total darkening of vision. The perception which itself transcends everything is beyond perception itself, and so It becomes insensible to everything that is outside It. For how can that be sensory which does not know its nature, its origin, its location, or the identity and manner of its object, and is unable to either conceive or perceive all these things?" Saint Symeon the New Theologian

"Whence, in what manner could I have learned that anyone who believes in You becomes incorporated into You and reflects the Godhead? Who will believe this? - He becomes blessed,

having become a blessed member of the blessed Godhead. Wondrous, I see In me the One I believe to be in heaven, I mean You, 0 Christ, my Creator and King." - Saint Symeon the New Theologian

"This Is how You, the Ineffable, the invisible, the One not to be touched, the unmoving One, the One always present in all things everywhere, filling everything manifest and conceal Yourself at every moment of the day and night. You come and go, You disappear and suddenly re-appear. You eliminated the darkness in me little by little. You dissipated the cloud. You washed away the blindness from the mind's eye, cleared and freed my mind's hearing, removed the veil of my insensibility. Moreover, You pacified every passion, each carnal pleasure by chasing them away from me altogether. Having led me to this state, You purified the heaven of all clouds. I call heaven the purified Soul in which You suddenly find Yourself, I do not know how, 0 condescension beyond words. You reveal Yourself like a sun, You who are present everywhere." - Saint Symeon the New Theologian

4. THE MIND

The mind is the organ responsible for collecting the perceptions of the sense organs. The mind collects, assesses, stores, and retrieves information sent to it by the eyes, the ears, the nose, the mouth, and the skin.

The mind is living, but it is not life itself. It can think and choose, but it must learn to bow itself to the life that gives it life.

If a person is not open to their true identity, the mind can believe that it is the centre of man and that it is the source of his life, and that it can make decisions for that man. These decisions are not in keeping with man's higher nature or divine self, because there is no consideration for the energy of the higher nature or soul. This is a very rudimentary way of living. We collect data from the senses, and we make decisions based on that data alone.

The mind is capable of keeping man alive by keeping the body away from harmful influences and attached to positive influences. This is how we are able to stay out of flames when we see them, and how we know we should eat food when we are hungry. But again, this is rudimentary. It is not the use of the fullest capabilities within man.

Images of perception, collected by senses and stored in the mind on a repeated basis, will be transferred from simple information and knowledge in the mind to impressions and feelings in the heart. That is, repetition takes things from the mind and places them in the heart. When we perceive something over a period of time, or perceive it repeatedly, we must make some form of impression or feeling about that thing.

Most childhood memories are images placed in the heart because of their repetition. The images move from the mind to the heart because of the frequency with which they occur. Other events perceived by the senses and placed in the mind may move to the heart because of the grandeur of what they represent. That is, a pivotal moment or a traumatic event may go into the heart immediately, as soon as it is placed in the mind.

5. HEART

The heart is the organ of feeling and intuition. It is at the small end of the funnel of the mind. Things will pass into the heart from the mind because of the energy they represent in terms of repetition or grandiosity (repeated events or grandiose events). When we say we have feelings about something, they are coming from the heart.

The heart is living, but it is not life itself. It can feel and choose, but must itself learn to bow to the life that gives it life.

Things that pass from the mind into the heart will begin to ferment there. The heart will allow feelings about things to grow. It is a place of growth.

We repeat the Jesus Prayer in order to enter into the heart from the mind. We must feel the mind drop into the heart.

We will feel pain in the heart as we approach the movement from the heart to the NOUS. This will be accompanied by light and then darkness, and the inward movement - a falling of the heart further into itself.

6. THE NOUS

The "nous" or eye of the soul is the organ at the centre of all organs. It is the very thing that gives life to all our person. It is the Image of God in us. It is the Divinity in us. It is a place, and if we are to be divinized, we must go there. Theosis occurs as we go there more and more.

When we enter into the NOUS we become attentive; that is, we begin to recognise that the mind is not alive of itself, but it gains its life from another centre; the heart is not alive of itself, but gains its life from another centre. The NOUS is the centre of our identity and it is our Life. The NOUS can transform our heart and mind and make them Like God, but we must step out of our minds and hearts and into the NOUS to have it transform us. We must become aware of the process of divinization if it is to happen, for awareness is the process. It is not a mental awareness of I AM, or a feeling of I AM, but it is both a mental awareness and a feeling that creates a state of I AM.

The NOUS is the New Man.

We become made-over into the LIKENESS of God by revisiting the IMAGE of God. When we revisit the Image of God in us, over and over, we could say we are carrying the Image of God to our mind and heart. By carrying the Image of God into the mind, we transform the mind. By carrying the Image of God into the heart, we transform the heart.

The NOUS is very small. One must become very small to enter it. One must collect all of the energy of the mind and squeeze it into a compact dot, and allow it to fall into the heart. Then, in the heart, one must collect all of the energy of the heart and squeeze it into a compact dot, and allow it to fall into the NOUS. Once this has happened, you will be in the centre of the world. You must sit there. You must go there often and it will transform you. Some say it makes you mad. This is divinization.

We become small by the humility that accompanies the continual praying of the name of Jesus.

7. AFTERWORD

When you have opened the eye of the soul, or begun to *"polish the Image of God in you"*, or *"entered into the NOUS"*, or *"become watchful"*, you begin to have the notion that this is who you are. You may realise I AM. This is the sacred space of the NOUS. It is the place where God is with you. It is a place of union with the Energies. If you are there, you will begin to catch a glimpse of the idea that *"the eye with which I see God is the same I with which God sees me"*.

May Jesus take us all to this place, and may He take us there often. May we taste and see that the LORD is good, and live in this goodness unto the Ages of Ages. Then shall we have attained Paradise. Then we shall have scaled the heights of Tabor

Pray that He shall send you a guide on your journey to the Promised Land

- Athanasios the sinner

GNOSIS
by Boris Mouravieff
STUDY AND COMMENTARIES ON THE ESOTERIC
TRADITION OF EASTERN ORTHODOXY

For the first time in English, this detailed study in contemporary terms of an ancient Christian spiritual tradition that illuminates the inner spiritual doctrines of the early church. The three volumes address the meaning of human life and history and its relation to divine purpose and cosmic processes, and provides practical information on the development of the heart and the transformation of spiritual energies. Reviewers said of this work:

"... the Orthodoxy of this book resides at a very deep level .. .one of those wonder-volumes that manages to rise above specific traditions to a plane of magnificent clarity... left me with a great sense of succor and hope." Timothy O'Neill, 'Gnosis' magazine.

"An astonishing display of brilliant and profound understanding of Fourth Way ideas..." Theodore J.Nottingham - 'In the Work'

VOL.I EXOTERIC CYCLE ISBN 1-872292-10-0 296 p pb
VOL.II MESOTERIC CYCLE, ISBN 1-872292-11-9 304 p pb
VOL.III ESOTERIC CYCLE, ISBN 1-872292-12-7 304 p pb
EACH $29.95 £19.50 $79.95 £54 SET OF THREE

Two books from Saint Theophan the Recluse

THE HEART OF SALVATION
The life and teachings of Theophan the Recluse, greatest of Russia's masters of inner Christianity, compiler of the fullest version of the Russian 'Philokalia'. The book draws on seven years of study in the ancient monasteries of the Middle East and is rooted in the richly practical spirituality of 19th Century Russia. It is of great practical significance to serious students of hesychastic spirituality.
ISBN 1-872292-02-X 208 pp pb $17.95 £10.95

THE PATH OF PRAYER
Also by St. Theophan the Recluse, a full introduction to the use of daily and liturgical prayer as a method of spiritual development.
ISBN 1-872292-14-3 PB $11.95, £6.95 HANDBOUND $16.95, £10.95

Other books and tapes offered by Praxis

WHO WRITES THE WAVES?

40 years of poems by Robin Amis. Often read in English poetry readings in the late sixties, these poems have an almost classical lyricism, and touch on the deepest questions of the inner life.
96 PAGES, HANDBOUND, $15.95. £9.95

TAPES FROM THE PHILOKALIA

Readings chosen by translator G.E.H. Palmer as a gift for his blind friend Julian Allen and read by Sergei Kadloubovsky. Taken from the original English translation of the 'Philokalia' published by Faber, these texts 'on watchfulness and holiness' are a meaningful and moving expression of the inner traditions of the early church fathers and a source of insight and solace to serious seekers of all traditions.
TWO 90 MIN. AUDIO TAPES : $19.95. £10.95

A DIFFERENT CHRISTIANITY

Robin Amis

After editing Mouravieff, Ouspensky and Theophan, Robin Amis, director of Praxis Institute, has finally written his own book, *A Different Christianity*, the distillation of more than 14 years of research into traditional sources of the Royal Way, a Christian spiritual discipline little known to the Western world. This work is now published by State University of New York Press, and is also available direct from PRAXIS.

"Amis here reveals the stream of the inner tradition from which Gurdjieff's teachings arose, in simpler form designed for a secular world and with additions borrowed from other inner traditions. This method is not one of obedience but of personal choice originating from a certain state of mind (sometimes called conscience) and resulting in a change of consciousness described as "waking up." In a striking anecdote resulting from his years of research, Amis informs us that, shortly before his death, Gurdjieff arranged for a group to travel to Mount Athos in an effort to reestablish contact with the tradition." Review by Theodore J. Nottingham in *Gnosis* magazine.

ISBN 0-7914-2751-1 384 PS, PB $19.95 £17.50
HARDBOUND $59.90 £49.95

by P.D.Ouspensky
THE COSMOLOGY OF MAN'S POSSIBLE EVOLUTION

The second series of O's lectures introducing his personal teaching - previously unpublished other than partially in *In Search*, where they were wrongly attributed to G.

ISBN 1-872-292-01-1 COSMOLOGICAL LECTURES PB £9.95
ISBN 1-872-292-00-3 WITH PSYCHOLOGICAL LECTURES: HARDCOVER £19.95

(Not for sale in N.America for copyright reasons.)

by Eugraph Kovalevsky
A METHOD OF PRAYER FOR MODERN TIMES

By the founder of the French Orthodox Church, a manual for methods of prayer of the Russian Church in a form suited to contemporary Western seekers.

ISBN 1-872292-18-6 146PP PB $16.95 £9.95

PRAXIS INSTITUTE PRESS - A DIVISION OF
PRAXIS RESEARCH INSTITUTE INC.
A non-profit corporation in the USA
2931 W.BELMONT AVE. CHICAGO, IL 60618 USA.
TEL: (773) 588 6294 FAX: (773) 588 3366
E-MAIL: praxis1@concentric.net
AND IN EUROPE - 5, DEVON PLACE, TOTNES,
DEVON TQ9 5AE, ENGLAND
TEL:01803 865250 FAX 01803 863599
E-MAIL: 73530.574@compuserve.com
SEE THE PRAXIS WEB PAGE ON:
http://www.concentric.net/~praxis1